THE PLAN OF THE BASILICA

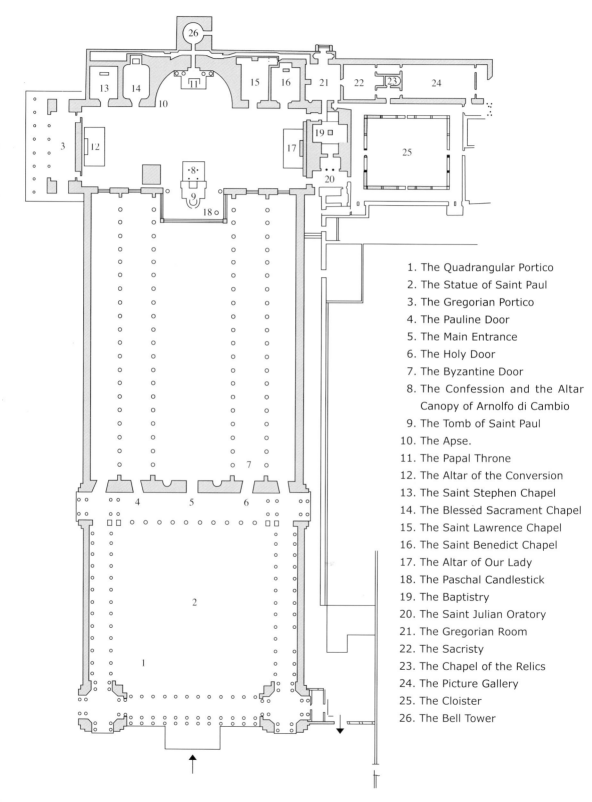

1. The Quadrangular Portico
2. The Statue of Saint Paul
3. The Gregorian Portico
4. The Pauline Door
5. The Main Entrance
6. The Holy Door
7. The Byzantine Door
8. The Confession and the Altar Canopy of Arnolfo di Cambio
9. The Tomb of Saint Paul
10. The Apse.
11. The Papal Throne
12. The Altar of the Conversion
13. The Saint Stephen Chapel
14. The Blessed Sacrament Chapel
15. The Saint Lawrence Chapel
16. The Saint Benedict Chapel
17. The Altar of Our Lady
18. The Paschal Candlestick
19. The Baptistry
20. The Saint Julian Oratory
21. The Gregorian Room
22. The Sacristy
23. The Chapel of the Relics
24. The Picture Gallery
25. The Cloister
26. The Bell Tower

The Papal Basilica of
Saint Paul
Outside the Walls

Libreria Editrice Vaticana

© Copyright 2008
Francesco Gioia

Texts and Captions
Anna Maria Cerioni
Roberto Del Signore
Andrea Cordero Lanza di Montezemolo

Translation
John A. Abruzzese
Edmund Power

Photographs
www.studiorifrazioni.it
ATS Italia Editrice Srl
© Biblioteca Apostolica Vaticana

Layout and Printing
Borgia Srl - Roma

Cover illustration
View of the Façade of the Basilica and Portico

Back cover illustration
Antoniazzo Romano, fresco of Saint Paul

ISBN 88-209-8043-6

Index

INTRODUCTION

After passing through the artistic iron gates, we enter a four-sided marble portico that defines the space around us, evoking a sense of calm and of harmony that somehow extends beyond the marble walls. At a subconscious level the frenetic life of the city outside is left behind. At the centre of the quadrangle rises a 19th century statue of St Paul: in solemn stance it reminds us that we are at the house of the Apostle who, with signal virtue, proclaimed his dedication to the Lord and affirmed, "*It is no longer I who live, but Christ who lives in me*" (Gal 2:20).

This pleasant mood accompanies us as we approach the narthex. Here, at the threshold of the great doors that manage to be at the same time majestic and austere, we find ourselves spellbound by the grandeur of the Basilica. This temple strikes us by its sheer enormity. There is a pervasive climate of silence that breathes the spirituality of the place.

In this hushed world with its suggestion of something mystical, we retain a sense of wonder for what man was able to create and for the message that he sought to leave behind for all those who enter. The precious gilded stucco of the ceiling, the coloured marbles and the solemn pillars give the impression of a marvellous musical instrument that chimes and choirs in harmony the refrain: Paul, we guard and celebrate him with pride. His mortal remains rest under the baldachin of Arnolfo di Cambio, under the Papal Altar, in that rough marble sarcophagus now partially revealed by the sensitive excavations conducted in the summer of 2006.

The Basilica of St Paul's outside the Walls, adorned, like the other major Basilicas, in accordance with the wishes of Pope Benedict XVI, with the title "Papal Basilica", now, for the first time in its history, has an Archpriest in addition to an Abbot (cf. *Motu Proprio of 31 May 2005*). It is the Sanctuary that has for twenty centuries jealously guarded the body of the Apostle of the Gentiles.

This booklet is published at the dawn of an historic event: the proclamation by Pope Benedict XVI of the Year of St Paul (28 June 2008 – 29 June 2009) to celebrate the bimillennium of the birth of the Apostle.

We prepare to live a jubilee Year of grace that will stir us to greater dedication in our lives as Christians and believers. Paul himself will certainly be present to help and encourage us; his prayer will continue to rise to the Lord: "*enlighten the eyes of our hearts, that we may know the hope to which we are called and the riches of our glorious inheritance in the saints*" (cf Eph 1:18).

Roma, 25 January 2008
The Conversion of St. Paul

Andrea Card. di Montezemolo
Archpriest
Papal Basilica of Saint Paul Outside the Walls

PRESENTATION

In 1988, the Pontifical Administration of the Patriarchal Basilica of Saint Paul sponsored the publication of a lengthy treatise on the Basilica dedicated to the Apostle of the Gentiles, under the auspices of Carlo Pietrangeli, General Director of Monuments, Museums and Pontifical Galleries, who was assisted by renowned scholars. Subsequently, in 1991, Anna Maria Cerioni and Roberto Del Signore were asked to compose an historical-artistic guidebook which appeared in five languages.

This second edition, available in the same five languages and utilizing the text of the initial edition, adds a new series of splendid photographs which permits a glimpse of the beauty of this imposing Basilica, reconstructed after the fire of 1823. The pilgrim is struck by the Basilica's size, the preciousness of its building materials and the various artifacts remaining from the old Basilica and adjoining Benedictine Abbey, among which are the mosaics, the Byzantine door, the Altar Canopy of Arnolfo, the Easter Candlestick and the superb Cosmati cloister.

The present publication, with its completely new photographic layout, has a twofold purpose: to increase devotion to the Apostle of the Gentiles and to make the beauty of the Basilica better known.

Many pilgrims visit the Basilica to pray at the tomb of the Apostle, located under the high altar. All experience the mysterious fascination of the unique figure of St. Paul, Imitator of Christ par excellence. As a courageous, untiring missionary, he carried the Gospel to the entire world of his time, pursuing a course of well over 7,800 kilometers on foot and 9,000 by ship. St. Paul himself states: "I have become all things to all men, that I might by all means save some" (1 Cor 9:23). Nothing could extinguish his apostolic zeal. For him, even difficulties were a source of joy, as he tells the Corinthians: "For the sake of Christ, I am content with weaknesses, insults, hardships, persecutions and calamities" (2 Cor 12:10).

For those who encounter him in the Basilica built in his honor, and also for those who in whatever way are engaged in his venture in life and spirit, all that remains is to accept St. Paul's invitation: "Be imitators of me, as I am of Christ" (1 Cor 11:1).

Roma, 25 January 2003
The Conversion of St. Paul

+ Francesco Gioia, *Archbishop*
Pontifical Administrator
of the Patriarcal Basilica of Saint Paul

1. An Historical Overview

The Basilica of Saint Paul Outside the Walls which stands on the via Ostiense about 2 kilometres from the Aurelian Walls, near the left bank of the Tiber is the second largest Roman church after the Vatican

The site, which has never ceased to be the destination of pilgrims and ordinary visitors is situated on the burial place of Saint Paul, the Apostle of the Gentiles. From the very first Holy Year in 1300, it has been included in the jubilee itinerary for indulgences and is one of the basilicas where the opening of the Holy Door is celebrated.

The present edifice was built over a period spanning more than a century, following the disastrous fire of July, 1823 which half-destroyed the grandiose ancient Basilica. Until that time, the building had remained substantially intact.

The construction of a place of worship on the site of the *cella memoriae* of Saint Paul the Liber Pontificalis attributes to the munificence of Constantine, marked from the 5th century by the two famous marble slabs bearing the inscription *"Paulo Apostolo Martyri"*. Saint Paul was buried in the small graveyard adjacent to *Via Ostiense*, not far from the area called *Ad Aquas Salvias* (known today as "Three Fountains"), the site of his martyrdom in 67 AD.

The apse of Constantine's Church was probably situated opposite the present one, standing on a road which is generally recognised to be the ancient route of the *Via Ostiense*. Since the Emperors Valentinian II, Theodosius and Arcadius decided to design a new place of worship, the original church must have been very modest in size. Building started some time between 384 and 386 and was completed under Honorius, as the mosaic inscription on the triumphal arch indicates:

"THEODOSIUS COEPIT PERFECIT HONORIUS AULAM / DOCTORIS MUNDI SACRATAM CORPORE PAULI."

The Basilica "of the Three Emperors", with its immense quadrangular portico with a fountain in the centre, had five entrances (at present, there are seven) and was quite similar to the 19th century reconstruction.

It was probably as a result of a natural disaster that the first restora-

Saint Paul, fresco of the workshop of Antoniazzo Romano (15th Century), from the lunette in the passageway between the Gregorian Room (Basilica entrance, Via Ostiense) and the Baptistry.

Giovanni Brun, View of the Nave of the Basilica of Saint Paul, end of 18th century (Biblioteca Apostolica Vaticana). Visible along the walls, above the famous series of papal portraits, are frescoes of scenes from the Acts of the Apostles and the Old Testament. The majority of them survived the fire, only to be destroyed during the rebuilding of the Basilica. The frescoes, attributed by Ghiberti to Pietro Cavallini, whose intervention during the last quarter of the thirteenth century left unaltered the iconographic programme of the old Leonine series, are primarily known because of copies which Cardinal Francesco Barberini had done in 1635. The paintings were executed along the wall in two parallel planes, each having twenty-two compartments. On the right are scenes from the Old Testament; on the left, stories from the Acts of the Apostles. Representations of the prophets appear between the windows above.

VEDUTA INTERNA DELLA BASILICA

tion took place in the middle of the 5th century under Leo I (440-461) This Pope also began to decorate with mosaics the recently fortified triumphal arch of the Basilica. The series of paintings on the walls of the nave, depicting scenes from the Old and New Testament (repainted by Cavallini at the end of the 13th century), and the beginning of the first series of papal portraits from Peter to Innocent I (401-417) are also attributed to him.

From then onwards, restoration and embellishments advanced in relation to each pope's constant devotion to the Apostle of the Gentiles and veneration for the Basilica erected in his honour. At the end of the 5th century, under Pope Symmachus (498-514), the apse, which was in bad condition, was restructured, the Confession decorated and some *habitacula* (lodging rooms) constructed to offer hospitality to the poor and pilgrims.

Gio: Brun Scul

S. PAOLO =

At the time of Gregory the Great (590-610)in all likelihood, work was carried out on the presbytery area, the floor of the transept was raised and connected to the nave by means of five steps.

A semi-circular crypt, probably later destroyed under the pontificate of Leo III (795-816), and the tomb containing the remains of the Apostle was also opened behind the high altar. Sergius I (687-701) later repaired the roof of the Basilica and renovated the *cubicula* (bedrooms) of the *habitacula* of Pope Symmachus mentioned above.

At the time of Hadrian I (772-795) work resumed, the lateral naves were restored and a new floor was laid in the atrium.

It was also Hadrian who embellished the Basilica with liturgical ornamentation. His successor, Leo III (795-816), continued his work and also had the roof repaired, a marble floor laid and saw to the restoration of the apse vault, which, as the *Liber Pontificalis* mentions, was decorated with a mosaic like the one in the Vatican. John VIII (872-882) surrounded the Basilica with sturdy walls to protect it from pirate-like raids similar to the devastating Saracen attack in 846, following what Leo IV (847-855) had done to the Vatican in 848-849. The exact development or extension of the small citadel, called Giovannipoli in honour of the Pope, is unknown. However, it must have been fortified well enough to later withstand the repeated attacks of the Emperor Henry IV in 1083-1084.

It was during the 11ᵗʰ century that two important works were added to the Basilica: the bell tower, built next to the north nave, near the façade, and the bronze door of the main entrance, forged in Constan-

tinople and donated by Pantaleone di Amalfi in 1070. In the meantime, Hildebrand of Soana, while Abbot at Saint Paul's and later to become Pope Gregory VII (1073-1085), reformed the monastery and restored the Church.

In 1115, the presbytery area was devastated by a fire and therefore Pope Innocent II (1130-1143) had a wall built on columns along the whole length of the transept so as to support the unsafe roof, thus dividing it into two small naves. Its greatest moment of splendour came for the Basilica during the 13th century and the first quarter of the 14th century, when, Nicola D'Angelo and Pietro Vassalletto made the Paschal Candlestick; the mosaic decoration of the bowl-shaped vault of the apse was carried out under Honorius III (1216-1227); the wonderful cloister was built (1208-1235); the cycle of paintings in the nave were carried out by Pietro Cavallini (which were to disappear during the 19th century rebuilding); Arnolfo di Cambio, *cum suo socio Petro* ("with his partner Peter") produced the priceless Altar Canopy; and, finally, the façade was decorated with a mosaic (1325). The Basilica was badly damaged and the bell tower and part of the portico were destroyed during the 1349 earthquake. Pope Clemente VI (1342-1352), however, quickly undertook the restoration project.

At the beginning of the 14th century, when Boniface IX (1389-1404)—whose statue stands in the cloister—realized that the Church was falling into ruin, the total amount of indulgence offerings was set aside for its repair, a practice which continued under Martin V (1417-1431). However, it was only in 1426 in response to a proposal by Cardinal Gabriele Condulmer, the future Eugene IV (1431-1447)that the work of restoring the Ostiense complex began.

The 16th century saw interventions by Gregory XIII (1572-1585) who had the presbytery area decorated with paintings and the Apostle's tomb surrounded by a balustrade for the 1575 Jubilee Year and Sixtus V (1585-1590) had the presbytery area restored and a coffered ceiling to the transept was added.

Under Clement VIII (1592-1605) new altars were erected, among them that of Saint Bridget and the high altar, attributed to Onorio Longhi. The Chapel of the Blessed Sacrament (today named in honour of Saint Lawrence) was erected by Carlo Maderno in 1619-1620 and decorated by Giovanni Lanfranco with frescoes and paintings of a Eucharistic theme.

In response to the request of Innocent X (1644-1655), Francesco Borromini's plan for the total restructuring of the Basilica can be dated to 1653, shortly before Innocent X had commissioned the Lombard ar-

chitect to restore Saint John Lateran. Two semi-circular porticoes were to be built, at both the front and the back. The Pamphilj Pope, however, could only able to start work on the new roof, later to be completed under Clement X (1670-1676). On 1st May 1724, the portico which had recently been erected suddenly collapsed, much to the embarrassment of the architect, Alessandro Specchi,. Antonio Canevari was immediately given orders by Pope Benedict XIII (1724-1730) to rebuild it for the approaching Holy Year celebration. In the course of work, the ancient narthex was destroyed and the surviving columns of the Palaeo-Christian quadrangular portico were removed.

The Chapel of the Crucifix (today named in honour of the Blessed Sacrament), housing the venerated 14th century crucifix attributed at the time to Pietro Cavallini, was rebuilt in the same year. Finally, in 1747, the apse mosaic from which some fragments were taken was restored thanks to Benedict XIV(on view in the room near the Sacristy). He also oversaw the restoration of the cycle of frescoes by Cavallini and the series of papal portraits which was continued and completed by the painter, Salvatore Monosilio, to include the reigning Pope.

2. THE 1823 FIRE AND RECONSTRUCTION

On the night between 15 and 16 July 1823, a terrible fire, caused by the carelessness of workers who were restoring the roof, ravaged the ancient Basilica. In no time whatsoever most of the building was destroyed. When the firemen arrived, they were confronted by "a spectacular sight [...] it was like a terrible Vesuvius, the lofty flames leapt higher than the highest mountains in their fatal dominion, this terrible accident could be seen for fifteen miles or more and every heart was filled with a sacred and penetrating horror" (C. Pietrangeli, *S. Paolo fuori le mura a Roma*, 1988, p. 67).

The outcome was extremely serious. The central nave suffered the greatest damage. The roof caved in–as did lateral naves and transept–, most of the left wall crumbled and several of the forty columns collapsed. Those columns which were still upright were irreparably damaged. The apse area, the triumphal arch (although it threatened to fall), the dividing colonnades and the external walls of the lateral naves, the façade with its portico and the bell tower still remained standing. While the transept walls seemed intact, the great dividing wall, erected by Innocent II (1130-1143) to support the roof, threatened to collapse.

Many of the works of art in the Basilica were also destroyed by the flames. Although, Cavallini's frescoes, the series of papal portraits, the mosaics of the triumphal arch and the bowl-shaped vault in the apse and Arnolfo's Altar Canopy survived, they were all in urgent need of restoration.

Among those who rushed to view the ruins which were extensively visually documented was the horrified and astonished Stendhal. In his work entitled *Roman Walks*, he describes it in the following manner: "I visited Saint Paul's the day after the fire. I had an impression of severe beauty, as sad as Mozart's music. The terrible, painful traces of the misfortune were still alive; the Church was still cluttered with half-burned, black smouldering beams; the trunks of the columns which were split from top to bottom threatened to fall down at any moment. The dismayed Romans had come out en masse to see the burned Church. It was one of the most overwhelming sights I had ever seen".

Pope Pius VII (1800-1823), who was at the time advanced in years and ailing (he died a little more than a month later on 20 August), never came to know of what had happened, as the Pope's most trusted collaborators and the secretary of State Cardinal Consalvi being the first had

wanted. His successor, Leo XII (1823-1829) therefore had arduous task of starting the rebuilding of the Basilica, elected on 28 October, he immediately dedicated himself to the task. The exceptional importance of the building and the agonizing dilemma posed by the extensiveness of the damage faced the architects with difficult decisions. Should the Basilica be rebuilt *in pristinum*, that is, maintaining the exact plan of the former one and reproducing the same architectural style, or should an entirely new building be created according to modern architectural theory?

What ensued was a heated debate, with many people offering various designs and written opinions.

Architects like Giuseppe Valadier and Pasquale Belli, scholars like Carlo Fea and Angelo Uggeri and ordinary citizens equally took part.

Of particular interest is Valadier's plan, of which three versions are known from drawings and engravings. A 90-degree rotation of the façade was proposed, placing it in the west end of the transept; the old transept was to become the nave of the new Basilica and opposite the old one a second apse was to be opened, while the lateral naves and the portico of the original façade were to be used to house ancient monuments and provide space for processions within the building.

Pasquale Belli and Andrea Alippi, in the meantime, began the urgent work of propping up the unsafe walls and closing off the two chapels dedicated to the Crucifix and the Blessed Sacrament, where religious services had continued.

After much debate, in September 1824, Giuseppe Valadier, willing to work for nothing as long as he could see his plan realized, was finally placed in charge of the rebuilding, with Salvi, Paccagnini and Alippi as his assistants.

Luigi Rossini, Interior of the Damaged Basilica, Viewed from the Entrance, 1823. The engraving, made shortly after the disastrous fire, appears with three others in the collection entitled "Roman Antiquities" in which the famed ruins are given the same importance as those of ancient Rome.

In order to face the immense expense estimated for what was to become the greatest construction site in Papal Rome in the 19th century, Leo XII issued his Encyclical letter Ad Plurimas Easque Gravissimas (25th January 1825) In the document, the Pope invited the bishops to promote a collection of offerings from the faithful to finance the rebuilding effort, much like Julius II had done for Saint Peter's. Reiterated by Gregory XVI (1831-1846) in 1840, this urgent appeal resulted in the sending of money (more than 400,000 *scudi* were collected) and precious materials, of which the gifts of the Viceroy of Egypt (alabaster columns) and Czar Nicolas I (blocks of malachite) are well-known.

On 23 November 1825, in response to the wishes of the Pope who had favoured the *in pristinum* rebuilding plan a few months earlier, the special Reconstruction Commission removed Valadier from his position and placed Belli in charge, with Pietro Bosio, Andrea Alippi and Pietro Camporese the Younger as his assistants. The great opportunity for a new architectural design was therefore lost and rebuilding was resumed according to outdated academic canons.

Although Belli conserved the old portico and façade, he destroyed most of the medieval remains.

However, the rather innovative idea of raising the nave floor was carried out by Luigi Poletti, who subsequently raised it approximately 90 centimetres.

The demolition of Galla Placidia's arch initiated rebuilding work, once the valuable mosaic had been removed (September 1826), it was later reconstructed on massive columns of Montórfano granite, erected in the Summer of 1829. After the dividing wall of the transept was torn down (1826), the mosaic of the bowl-like vault in the apse was restored (1828). The west walls of the transept and those of the central nave were demolished at the same time, thus the Cavallini frescoes were lost.

As the first of the eighty columns of the naves was being erected Gregory XVI ascended the papal throne in 1831. His numerous visits to the building site are testimony to his keen interest in the Ostiense building. Two years later, Luigi Poletti from Modena (1792-1869) succeeded Belli in directing the project, assisted by Bosio, Camporese and Virginio Vespignani (1808-1882).

Finally, after a series of mishaps, on 5 October 1840, the Pope was able to solemnly consecrate the Altar of Confession over which rose the restored Altar Canopy of Arnolfo. The transept, isolated from the naves, was to serve as the Basilica for the time being. By that date, the Blessed Sacrament and the Crucifix Chapels had already been restored and the Saints Stephen and Benedict Chapels, whose decoration was nearing completion, had been built next to them. The portico, which had served as a façade to the Basilica for a long time, on the west end of the transept, was also finished. The construction of the bell tower, behind the apse, had begun (which would be completed in 1860), and fifty-eight columns were standing in the naves.

Archaeological discoveries were also made in the course of the work. In 1850, Vespignani undertook some surveying around the tomb of Saint Paul and Belloni discovered the apse of the early Constantine Basilica.

In the pontificate of Pius IX (1846-1878) work continued so swiftly that the Pope was able to consecrate the new Basilica on 10 December 1854 in a lavish ceremony. Over the Altar of Confession, above Arnolfo's Altar Canopy, rose a still-more-imposing architectural canopy which was demolished in 1912 (the four columns are now part of the internal side of the Basilica's façade).

The new façade took many years to reach completion although its plan had been approved in 1850. Filippo Agricola had drawn the designs for the mosaic in 1856, but the work on the narthex continued between 1873 and 1884 under Virginio Vespignani, the newly appointed person in charge of rebuilding, who also started the construction of the portico envisioned by Poletti.

In 1857 The decoration of the walls of the naves and transept began with the continuation and updating of the portraits of the popes and the painting of *Scenes from the Life of Saint Paul,* done by numerous artists of the Roman School.

Work slowed down considerably After the unification of Italy and came to be completely suspended from 1884 to 14 March 1890, when the first stone of the quadrangular portico was laid. The portico was completed in 1928, as designed by Guglielmo Calderini, following an unfavourable judgment on Vespignani's plan.

The historical-artistic story of the reconstruction of the *Ostiense* Basilica, lasting a century, concludes with the building of the quadrangular portico, the erection of Antonio Maraini's bronze door in 1931 and Arnaldo Foschini's construction, in the same period, of the Baptistry in a room adjacent to the south transept.

3. The Location

The Basilica is situated between the *Via Ostiense*, which almost touches the eastward-facing apse, and the left bank of the Tiber, elements which, since antiquity, have greatly figured in the Basilica's relationship to the city of Rome in a dialectic and symbolic way. The construction of the Rome-Civitavecchia railway line (1862) and the raising of the banks of the Tiber (1930) during the last two centuries changed this situation. The former interrupted the linear view of the Basilica walls and the latter, with the consequent disappearance of the Almone torrent, brought an end to the Basilica's often dramatic relationship with water.

Above:
The Basilica and its
quadrangular portico,
with the top of the
bell tower in the
rear.

Right:
The Basilica as seen
from inside
the cloister.

4. THE QUADRANGULAR PORTICO

In front of the façade, the majestic portico, was built by Guglielmo Calderini between 1890 and 1928, developing Luigi Poletti's initial plan which had been modified at his death in 1869 by Virginio Vespignani. Since ancient times a porticoed atrium existed in front of the Basilica. The construction undertaken by Calderini, however, is entirely different and much larger. The northern and southern sections of the present portico, whose sides, which are closed off on the outside by travertine-covered walls, measure 70 metres in length. The western side, on the other hand, opens onto the façade in a series of thirteen arches. At each corner monumental propylaea join the sides of the portico. The imposing one hundred and fifty columns are arranged in a single line in the narthex, in two lines in the northern and southern sides and in three in the main front section, where paintings in the thirteen lunettes depict Christ giving his blessing, flanked by the Apostles. Multi-coloured marbles decorate the portico's side walls and they are adorned with painted medallions depicting the symbols of the four Evangelists and Paleo-Christian symbols (vines, doves, an orb, deer, peacocks, etc).

The massive statue of Saint Paul by Giuseppe Obici (1807-1878), located in the center of the quadrangular portico.

View of the façade and the quadrangular portico. On the upper part of the façade appear mosaics which were done between 1854 and 1874 by the Vatican Mosaic Studio, based on drawings by Filippo Agricola and Nicola Consoni. They depict the prophets Isaiah, Jeremiah, Ezekiel and Daniel, the Agnus Dei and Christ with his hand raised in blessing, flanked by the Apostles Peter and Paul. Part of the vestibule's rich, painstakingly-done decoration are the doors of the three main entrances (on the right is the Holy Door). The niches contain statues of Saints Peter and Paul by Gregorio Zappalà (1833-1908).

5. The Bronze Door

The sculptor Antonio Maraini (1886-1963) made the Bronze Door of the Basilica's main entrance between 1929 and 1931, as indicated by the inscription at the bottom, where the dedication to the two Princes of the Apostles also appears.

The then abbot of Saint Paul's, Bl. Ildefonso Schuster (1880-1954), devised the door's iconographical plan based on the glory coming from the Apostles' preaching in the sign of the cross. Measuring an imposing 7.48 metres high and 3.35 metres wide, the entire area is signed by a huge cross, composed of vine branches in silver damascening in which, suspended in ovals of lapislazuli, are engravings of the Apostles along the central edges of the double doors, and symbols of the Evangelists on the crosspiece. In the uppermost panels are the Church's insignia (left) and the City of Rome (right). Each of the ten panels, five on each of the doors, depicts an event which took place in the city, with the exception of the two central panels dominat-

Right and page 24: Details from the bronze door: The Giving of the Keys to Peter and The Founding of the Apostolic See; and St. Paul's Arrival in Rome as a Prisoner.

ed by the silver figure of Christ. These panels represent crucial moments in the lives of the two Apostles: *Christ Giving the Keys to Saint Peter and Saint Paul's Conversion on his Way to Damascus.*

On the right, progressing from bottom to top, are events from the life of Saint Paul: *Saint Paul Reaching Rome and his Welcome by the Roman Faithful; Saint Paul Making Conversions in Rome; The Conversion of the Centurion*; and *The Beheading of Saint Paul*; on the left, in the same order, are those related to the life of Saint Peter: *Saint Peter Baptizing in the Catacombs; The Founding of the Apostolic See; "Domine Quo Vadis?"*; and *The Crucifixion of Saint Peter.*

6. THE HOLY DOOR

The new Holy Door, which is located to the right of the Basilica's main entrance and composed of two gilded bronze panels, was dedicated on 30 June 2000, replacing the former wooden one. With a height of 3.71 metres, a width of 1.82 metres, and weighing 800 kilograms, the door has a Trinitarian theme, conceived and executed by the sculptor Enrico Manfrini.

On the left, in the upper section, the mercy of God the Father is portrayed in the Parables of the Prodigal Son and the Good Samaritan; on the right, this attribute is reflected in the Pope who, in the foreground, extends his arms to embrace the poor and the sick.

On the left, in the middle section, God the Holy Spirit descends on the Virgin Mary and the Apostles at Pentecost, while, on the right, his work continues in the evangelization of peoples, particularly through Saint Paul, who undergoes martyrdom in the lower, left-hand corner.

The Redemption of humanity is accomplished by God the Son, through his death on the cross, on the left, in the lower section; on the right, his work of salvation is continued through the ages by the bishops who guide humanity to the font of life.

Finally, at the base, the two-line inscription is a greeting to all visi-

tors of the Pauline Basilica, wishing them the gift of peace and eternal salvation: *Ad sacram Pauli cunctis venientibus aedem – sit pacis donum perpetuoque salus* ("May the gift of peace and eternal salvation be granted to all who come to Paul's holy temple").

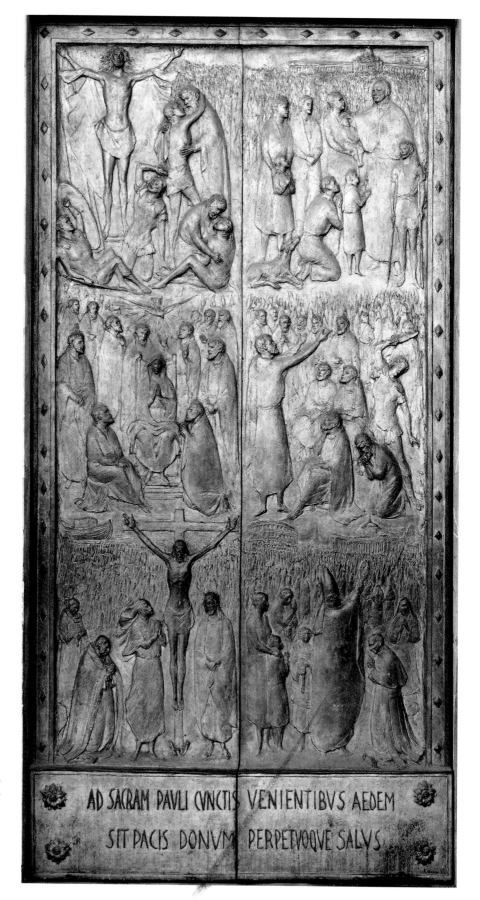

The Holy Door by the sculptor Enrico Manfrini.

7. THE INTERIOR

The Basilica is divided into five naves, following the plan of a Tau cross, by four rows of twenty columns and a raised transept, and measures 131 metres in length, 65 metres in width and 30 metres in height.

Begun by Pasquale Belli, work on the interior continued from 1831 to 1854 under Luigi Poletti, who, until his death in 1869 was in charge of the work of restoration from 1833. The central nave is bound by forty archivolted columns of Baveno granite with white Carrara marble Corinthian capitals. Above the frieze-like area of papal portraits, between Corinthian pilasters, murals depicting scenes from the life of Saint Paul alternate with arched windows. Six alabaster columns donated by the Egyptian Viceroy, Mohamed Alì, in 1840 decorate the inside of the Basilica's façade. The two central columns bear the massive marble coat-of-arms of Pius IX (1846-1878), the work of Giosuè Meli, which is supported by two, winged figures sculptured by Ignazio Iacometti and Salvatore Revelli. The floor of the naves and of the transept, incorporating materials recovered from the ancient Basilica, resembles an immense carpet of precious marbles .In the rich, gold coffered ceilings, the coats-of-arms of the Popes associated with the history of the building appear. Along the walls of the central nave, the two smaller naves and the transept are large arched windows, inset with thin panels of alabaster, donated by King Faud I of Egypt. In the walls of the two outer naves, in massive niches, are the statues of ten Apostles (five on each side) which, together with those of Saint Peter and Saint Paul on pedestals in the central nave, were sculptured in 1882 by artists such as A. Allegretti, F. Fabi-Altini, E. Gallori and E. Maccagnani, who followed exacting academic theory.

Following pages: View of the interior of the Basilica with the double colonnade of Corinthian columns.

The solemn and majestic central nave, viewed from the transept.

Details from the wooden ceilings of the transept and the nave.
Above: The coat-of-arms of Gregory XVI (1831-1846).
Below: The coat-of-arms of Pius IX (1846-1878).

8. THE BYZANTINE DOOR

Used in the main entrance of the Basilica before the fire, in 1967 the splendid Byzantine Door, occupied the place of the Holy Door. It was commissioned by the Consul Pantaleone di Amalfi, as the Latin and Greek inscriptions indicate (portrayed in one of the panels) in Constantinople and was produced in 1070 by an artist named Teodoro. For a long time, Staurachio, who was only involved in its casting, was thought to be the artist.

In the 1823 fire, the double doors suffered serious damage, they are divided into six vertical strips with 54 panels, some of which were partially restored in 1965-66 (four were lost).

The panels develop a complex iconographical plan with twelve Christological scenes (from the Nativity to Pentecost), the twelve Apostles and scenes of their martyrdom, twelve prophets, two eagles, two crosses and two panels with two dedicatory inscriptions in Latin, all done in silver damascening.

The door is a rather fine example of the artistry existent at that time.

Details from the Byzantine Door: The Martyrdom of Saint Peter and the Martyrdom of St. Paul.

Key to the Iconographic Subjects on the Byzantine Door

Left Side

1. The Annunciation
2. The Birth of Jesus Christ
3. The Presentation
4. The Baptism of Jesus Christ
5. The Transfiguration
6. The Entry into Jerusalem
7. The Crucifixion
8. The Deposition from the Cross
9. The Resurrection
10. The Apparition to the Apostles
11. The Ascension
12. Pentecost
13. The Cross
14. The Inscription *Tu quoque*
15. The Martyrdom of Saint Paul
16. Jesus, Saint Paul, Saint Pantaleon
17. The Martyrdom of Saint Peter
18. St. Peter
19. The Martyrdom of Saint Andrew
20. Saint Andrew
21. The Burial of Saint John
22. Saint John the Theologian
23. The Martyrdom
    of Saint Bartholomew
24. Saint Bartholomew
25. The Eagle
26. Saint Thomas
27. The Martyrdom of Saint Thomas

Right Side

*Details from
the Byzantine Door:
The Crucifixion
of Christ and Saint Peter.*

9. WOODEN MODEL OF THE BASILICA (SCALE 1:50)

Restored, illuminated and mounted on a mobile support, the wooden model of the Basilica, was situated at the entrance of the right lateral nave. The architect Poletti, to whom reconstruction of the Basilica Ostiense had been entrusted, had it done by Serafino Colagiacomi on a scale of 1:50 in 1844.

Representing the project of Luigi Poletti for the reconstruction of the complex of Saint Paul and including the Basilica, the Quadri –portico, constructed at the end of the nineteenth century by Guglielmo Calderini using different architecture, and the octagonal baptistry which was never constructed. It is divided in two parts along the longitudinal axis, to allow observation from in-

side. It is made up of four different kinds of wood: oak for the joint elements and the base frame, larch and poplar for the architectural structure and cherry for the turned and moulded elements.

It was necessary to summarize, in the yard, what had been done and what had to be discussed, and with regards to the inside of the Basilica. It remained, however, the represen-

tation of an incomplete idea: neither Gregory XVI nor his successor wanted to undertake the entire project.

Attribution to Serafino Colagiacomi and the date of 1844 of the model result from the pencil annotation on the plate inserted in the base.

In 1866 the wooden model was still to be found at the Basilica yard. In 1910 it was given by Calderini to the Abbot of Saint Paul's for exhibition to the public in one of the halls of the new gallery, where it remained until the thirties. It was then deposited in various warehouses until it was finally settled in the hall adjoining the Sala Barbo in 1983. It was restored in 2003, now illuminated and mounted on a mobile support it is situated at the entrance of the Basilica in the right lateral nave.

The model (130x203x517 cm) made of precious woods, creates particular interest, as it demonstrates the solutions not carried out proposed by the architect from Modena. The prospect was dominated by the bulk of the Baptistry on the central plan and with octagonal tibury, surmounted by a cupola. The entrances, however should have opened onto the centre of the two sides. The vertical section of the bell tower shows the audacious internal solution of the spiral staircase.

The model is seen with a passage in the central part, where opportune illumination allows the architectural solutions adopted to be appreciated. At the same time, through a sheet of crystal placed on the floor, it is possible to see some of the remains of the burial ground of the IV and VI which exist under the Basilica.

10. The Papal Portraits

The series of Papal Portraits, above the naves and transept, reconstructed from the famous series in the ancient Basilica begun in the 5th century by Pope Leo the Great (440-461), continued by Cavallini at the end of the 13th century and followed by Benedict XIV (1740-1758) during the work of preparation for the Holy Year 1750. Of the original series, the forty-one surviving portraits, documented in the Vatican Latin Codex 4407, are now kept in the adjoining Abbey. In May, 1847 Pius IX (1846-1878) instructed that the work of replacing the old series was to be done in mosaic rather than fresco. Filippo Agricola, the Director of the Vatican Mosaic Studio, was assigned the task of determining the papal likenesses. Of the many painters involved in the work, some of whom were employed in the series of frescoes on scenes from the life of Saint Paul, for example, Bompiani, Canterani, De Rossi, Trojetti, Podesti and Sozzi. Work was completed on the oil-painting models in two years, presently kept in the Fabric of Saint Peter's, while their realization in mosaic continued to 1876. The series has been updated with each new Pope.

11. THE PAULINE SERIES

Set between Corinthian pilasters and above the Papal Portraits, thirty-six frescoes, depicting *Scenes from the Life of Saint Paul* from the Acts of the Apostles, alternate with windows along the walls of the central nave and transept. Commissioned by Pius IX (1846-1878) in 1857 this series of frescoes was to replace those of Cavallini which had been destroyed. It took only three years and a group of twenty-two artists to complete the work, including Francesco Podesti, Pietro Gagliardi, Carlo Gavardini, Francesco Coghetti and Francesco Grandi, all worthy of mention because of the quality of their work. Each painting is framed in marble; above are paintings of putti holding a shield bearing the Latin title of the scene. The scenes begin in the transept to the right of the apse, in the first set of pilasters, continue in the nave and conclude in the left transept and are arranged in chronological order.

The scenes are as follows: *Saul, Persecutor of Christians, Present at the Martyrdom of Saint Stephen* and *The Conversion of Saul*, both paintings by Pietro Gagliardi (1809-1890); *Ananias Lays Hands on Saul Who Receives the Virtues of the Holy Spirit* and *Ananias Baptizes Saul* by Francesco Podesti (1800-1895); *Paul Preaches in Damascus and Paul Flees from Damascus* by Guglielmo De Sanctis (1829-1911); *Paul Among the Apostles at the Council of Jerusalem* by Nicola Consoni (1814-1884); *The Consecration of Paul and Barnabas, Paul Converts Sergius, Proconsul of Paphos, Paul and Barnabas in Lystra* and *The Stoning of Paul in Lystra* by Cesare Mariani (1826-1901); *Paul's Vision in Troas* and *Paul Exorcises a Young Girl in Philippi* by Luigi Cochetti (1802-1884); *Paul and Silas Are Flogged in Philippi* by Vincenzo Morani (1809-1870); *Paul Converts the Jailer in Philippi* by Giuseppe Sereni; *Paul's Speech in the Areopagus of Athens* by Giovan Battista Pianello (1812-after 1866); *Paul in Corinth* by Domenico Tojetti (1807-1892); *The Converted Ephesians Burn their Scrolls* by Casimiro De Rossi; *Paul Brings the Young Eutychus Back to Life* by Natale Carta (1790-1884); *Paul Leaves for Miletus* by Marcello Sozzi; *The Prophecy of Agabus* by Roberto Bompiani (1821-1908); *Paul and James in Jerusalem,* by Cesare Dies (1830-after 1884); *Paul is Expelled from the Temple in Jerusalem* and *Paul's Speech to the People of Jerusalem* by Francesco Grandi (1831-1891); *Paul Declares Himself to be a Roman and Escapes Flogging in Jerusalem* by Natale Carta; *Paul's Vision in Jerusalem and Paul before Felix in Caesarea* by Domenico Bartolini; *Paul's Shipwreck in Cauda and Paul and The Viper in Malta* by Achille Scaccioni; *Paul Cures the Father of Publius, Prince of Malta* by Nicola Consoni; *Paul Meets the Christians of*

Rome on the Appian Way and Paul in Rome by Carlo Gavardini; *Paul's Elevation to the Third Heaven and Peter and Paul in the Mammertine Prison* by Francesco Coghetti (1802-1875); *Peter and Paul Embrace before their Martyrdom and The Martyrdom of Saint Paul* by Filippo Baldi.

Filippo Balbi, Peter and Paul Embrace Before Their Martyrdom.

12. THE MOSAICS

The mosaic of the triumphal arch, called the mosaic of Galla Placidia, after the sister of Emperor Honorius was the patron of work, was made under the pontificate of Saint Leo the Great (440-461), at the same time as the one in the Basilica of Saint Mary Major.

Comparing it with the mosaic work in the Church of Saints Nereus and Achilleus, one can see that between the 8th and 9th centuries the mosaic work was completely redone. Unfortunately, due to various insufficient attempts at restoration, the present mosaic does not reflect its ancient splendour. In the central *clipeus* Christ is giving a blessing, flanked by two angels and symbols of the Evangelists. The Twenty-Four Elders from the Book of Revelation are portrayed, twelve on each side, with the Apostles Peter and Paul appearing below each group. The triumphal arch was rebuilt on two massive columns of Montórfano granite (14 metres high),after it was seriously damaged in the 1823 fire, after removing the mosaic and later replacing it in 1853.

A part of the mosaic decoration from the façade of the ancient Basilica was placed on the reverse side of the triumphal arch; the remaining parts were incorporated in the transept, on both sides of the apse mosaic. The mosaic which was commissioned by Pope John XXII (1316-1334) in 1325, and yet again was attributed by Ghiberti to Pietro Cavallini. Due to the extensive 19th century restoration work and the fact that the mosaic was in a deteriorated state before the fire, no conclusive analysis of style can be carried out with certainty

In ancient times the mosaic on the façade was divided as follows: the *clipeus* was in the tympanum, supported by two angels, with Christ giving a blessing and the symbols of the four Evangelists, two on either side. Mosaics of Saint Paul, a Madonna and Child, Saint John the Baptist and Saint Peter appeared in the lower part, between the windows.

As a consequence of the fire in the Basilica, the great mosaic in the bowl-like vault of the apse also suffered great damage; indeed almost the entire mosaic was replaced using little of the ancient tesserae. What remain are a few original fragments portraying the heads of the apostles and bird-designs which can be seen in areas adjoining the Basilica. The apse mosaic was made in the second and third decade of the 13th century by Venetian workmen called to Rome by Pope Honorius III (1216-1227), a fact confirmed by both documentation and by the affin-

Following pages: Detail from the reverse side of the triumphal arch.

GREGO
OPVS A
AN MI

Apse Mosaic commissioned by Honorius III and executed between 1220 and 1230.

ity in style with the mosaics of Saint Mark's Basilica in Venice. The mosaic work in Saint Paul's, together with that in the apse of the Vatican, marked the resumption of a great mosaic tradition in the city which would culminate at the end of the century with work in the major Roman Basilicas.

In the apse, Christ is seated on his throne, in the centre, and Pope Honorius III prostrate at his feet, with Saint Peter and Saint Andrew to his left, and, to his right, Saint Paul and Saint Luke. The figures stand in field resplendent with flowers and various animals. Beneath is a representation of the *Hetimasia* (the

empty throne with the cross and the instruments of Christ's passion), flanked by angels. Between the angels, at their feet, are seven almost undetectable figures, five representing the Holy Innocents and two kneeling characters from that time: Adinolfo, the Sacristan, and Giovanni Caetani, the Abbot. Apostles and Saints appear at the sides: on the right, James, Bartholemew, Thomas, Simon, Matthias and Mark; and, on the left, John, Philip, Matthew, James the Younger, Thaddaeus and Barnabas.

From the base of the throne to the representation of the *Hetimasia* and the figure of Pope Honorius III, which is the central part of the mosaic, is in all certainty original.

Positioned along the apse walls are memorial tablets with the names of various people who took part in the consecration of the Basilica. Having come from all corners of the earth, the participants assembled in Rome on 10 December 1854 for the procla-

mation of the dogma of the Immaculate Conception: the entire College of Cardinals, the Patriarch of Alexandria and a grand total of 140 bishops. In the centre stands the rich marble throne designed by Poletti, on the back of which is a relief by Pietro Tenerani, depicting *Christ Giving the Keys to Saint Peter*.

Below:
The triumphal arch and the apse area.
Opposite:
The apse vault with the papal cathedra.

Fragments of the apse
mosaic removed after
the 1823 fire and
presently kept in the
Gregorian Room next to
the sacristy of the
Basilica: apostle's head,
perhaps Saint Simon
(above); apostle's head
(below).

13. THE TOMB OF SAINT PAUL

The archaeological area of the tomb of Saint Paul is visible, in the area of the confessional, through two adjoining openings, the first in elevation, facing the Papal Altar, protected by a metal grating and the second on the floor, protected by a sheet of glass.

In 2006 the central part of the Constantine Apse was brought to light so as to meet the floor dimension. One can see how the whole apse area has been filled with a concrete cast of 1,60m in width, equal to the difference in the level of the floor between the Constantine building (320-330 circa) and the building of the Three Emperors (390). In the centre of this foundation plateau, which was necessary to support the Constantine Presbytery, was an altar structure which contained the

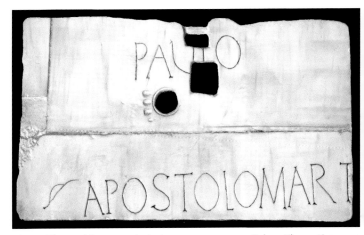

Above: The marble slab from the tomb of Saint Paul (4th-5th century) below the high altar.

A plaster reproduction is in the adjoining Abbey's Pinocoteca.

Below: The grating looking on the tomb of Saint Paul.

sarcophagus of Saint Paul, of the same dimensions of the other altars which succeeded the same Confessional.

Informative Text Relative To Making Saint Paul's Tomb Visible

During the Great Jubilee of 2000, many pilgrims, coming from all over the world to pay homage with their devotion to the Apostle, asked to see his burial site. The decision to carry out intensive investigation with the aim of identifying his burial site was therefore made.

The archaeological inspection carried out in 2002-2003 in the Confessional area allowed important progress to be made in the Constantine and Theodisian Basilica and the exact site of Saint Paul's sarcophagus to be known.

From May 2nd to November 17th 2006 the project to make Saint Paul's Tomb visible was completed. After having dismantled the Altar of the martyr Saint Timothy (v century) in the area of the hypogeum, on the west side of the Confessional, a tunnel was dug which allowed the side of the great Sarcophagus to be seen, under the Papal Altar. To increase visibility of the sarcophagus the opening was widened to 0,70m of the room. The archaeological Tomb is today visible through two adjoining openings: the first, vertical and protected by a metal grating, allows the side of the sarcophagus to be seen, the second, on the floor, allows the early Constantine Apse to be seen through a sheet of glass. The Sarcophagus is of the following dimensions: 2,55m in length, 1,25 in width, 0,97 in height and the cover is about 30cm thick.

Tomb of St Paul: Behind the grille, it is possible to see the side of the unpolished marble sarcophagus that contains the remains of St Paul.

14. THE ALTAR CANOPY

Arnolfo di Cambio is the author of the splendid Gothic Altar Canopy which rises above the papal altar, so called, because only the Pope can celebrate mass there (on very rare occasions also the Abbot of Saint Paul's). Due to the damage it suffered in the 1823 fire, that is, the calcination of the four porphyry support columns (later replaced) and the semi-destruction of some of the decorative elements of the small roof, the Altar Canopy was dismantled, restored and then remounted in its original position. It was discovered, during this process that Arnolfo had used ancient blocks of marble for his work and some of these bore inscriptions.

Mounted on the richly ornate capitals of four porphyry columns are-trefoil ogival arches, surmounted by triangular tympana with pinnacles at the sides and decorated with angels bearing a small rosette in a mosaic background. The bas-reliefs in the spraddles portray Adam and Eve, the Offering of Cain and Abel, Abbot Bartholomew offering the Altar Canopy to Saint Paul and a scene with two unidentified characters.

Between the small columns, in the corner niches, are statues of Saints Peter, Paul, Timothy and Benedict .In the centre, the Canopy's roof has a small shrine with a spire and pinnacles at each corner. The inter-nal sections are adorned with rich mosaics, including animals within roundels, some of which are flanked by canthari, while four, sometimes-boldly-foreshortened angels with candlesticks and thuribles are placed in the springer-corners of the vault. On the front, facing the nave, inscriptions testify to the fact that the Altar Canopy was built in 1285 by Arnolfo di Cambio, who was commissioned by Bartholomew, Abbot of the monastery from 1282-1297. A certain Pietro, known as "his partner," served as his assistant. In the past, he was thought to be Pietro Cavallini, but recent scholarship has identified him as Pietro di Oderisio. The hand of each man is distinguishable in the work as well as that of the assistants of the workshop. Apart from the general style, the small corner statues and other minor elements can be attributed to Arnolfo in all certainty. Due to its innovative sculptural language and architectural elements which bear novel Gothic features, the Altar Canopy of Saint Paul's—a forerunner to the one in Saint Cecilia's in Trastevere also by Arnolfo—was the beginning of a new artistic tradition, making Rome one of the foremost centres of art in Italy at the end of the 13th century with works carried out by Jacopo Torriti, Pietro Cavallini, Giotto and Arnolfo di Cambio.

Left: The Altar
Canopy with the
artists' names
and the dedication
to its commissioner.
Right: An angel with
candlestick in the
interior of the vault.

15. The Paschal Candlestick

Designed to hold the Easter Candle and to be placed near the altar in *cornu evangelii*, this type of candlestick has been a fundamental element of the Holy Saturday Liturgy since the 10th century. A unique example, the one in Saint Paul's, is a splendid example of the craftsmanship of marble cutters who created their own sculptural school in Rome between the 11th and 13th centuries. Its imposing character comes from both its colossal size (5.60 metres in height) and from the fact that its surface is completely carved. Subdivided horizontally into six sections, the tall shaft, stands on a base of alternating female and animal figures, some of the latter bearing human faces. The first section is decorated with plant and animal motifs; the last two sections bear plant arabesques; and those in-between portray the following scenes taken from Christ's Passion and Resurrection: *Christ before Caiphas, The*

Mocking of Christ, Christ before Pilate, Pilate Washing his Hands, The Crucifixion, The Resurrection and *The Ascension*. At the top, the huge cup meant to support the candle is supported by a ring of monstrous animals. As well as the developing Romanesque culture of the time, it is clearly consistent with Paleo-Christian art traditions; it also stands in succession to the decorative forms of the spiral columns of antiquity. Written below the series of scenes from Christ's life, are the names of the two artists responsible for the work: Nicola D'Angelo, who in all probability was responsible for the general design of the work, and Pietro Vassalletto, both members of important families of marble-carvers. This information is of particular importance in dating the work between the end of the 12th century and the beginning of the 13th and therefore creates a reference point in the history of Roman sculpture.

Detail:
The Crucifixion.

16. THE TRANSEPT

Two identical altars stand at the ends of the transept, composed of four Corinthian columns of *paonazzetto* marble which support an architrave with an inscription. On the right is the altar of Our Lady of the Assumption where a statue of Saint Benedict by Filippo Gnaccarini and one of Saint Scholastica by Felice Baini flank the mosaic done by the Vatican Mosaic Studio—a reproduction of the *Assumption of Our Lady,* believed to be from Monteluce, done by Giulio Romano and Penni, based on a drawing by Raphael now kept in the Vatican Picture Gallery. On the left is the altar of the Conversion of Saint Paul with a statue of Saint Gregory the Great by Francesco Massimiliano Laboureur, pupil of Thorvaldsen, and one of Saint Bernard, done by Achille Stocchi in 1836. Vincenzo Camuccini's painting of *The Conversion of Saint Paul* is above the altar. Of considerable value are the two altars, composed of malachite (donated by Czar Nicholas I) and lapis lazuli and supported at their corners by gold-plated, bronze angels. The four chapels off the transept, each with a different plan and construction date, are united in sharing the same rich, multi-coloured doors built in 1928 by the architect, Foschini.

The altar of the Assumption.

17. THE SAINT STEPHEN CHAPEL

Built by Poletti during the work done on the transept and dedicated to the first martyr who, in the Acts of the Apostles, is responsible for St. Paul's conversion is the Chapel of Saint Stephen. In part utilizing materials from the ancient Basilica, the marble work was close to completion in 1847. The walls of the rectangular Chapel are divided by pilasters of red granite, resting on a high, base-board moulding of African breccia marble. These pilasters are topped by Corinthian capitals with precious marble panels in between. The statue of Saint Stephen on the altar is the work of Rinaldo Rinaldi (1793-1873), a mediocre disciple of Canova. Two altar-pieces, commissioned by Gregory XVI in 1845, are in the centre of the side walls. The one on the left depicts *Saint Stephen Condemned by the Sanhedrin* by Francesco Coghetti and the one on the right portrays *The Stoning of Saint Stephen* by Francesco Podesti.

The Chapel of St. Stephen.

18. THE BLESSED SACRAMENT CHAPEL

The altar wall; Rigth, The revered wooden statue of Saint Paul.

The Blessed Sacrament Chapel was rebuilt for the 1725 Jubilee Year to house the venerated 14th century, wooden Crucifix thought then to be the work of Pietro Cavallini. Having survived the fateful fire, the Chapel maintains its original baroque form: a rectangular plan with concave angles, straight apse and eight wall niches. Attributed by Vasari to Cavallini, the wooden Crucifix, hangs above the altar. However, as a consequence of the meticulous restoration work done to the Crucifix from 1972-1974, during which the original polychrome work was retraced, it is now agreed that the work belongs to the Sienese school active at the beginning of the 14th century. The niches are occupied by statues: four golden stucco angels are in the side niches; and in the corner ones, next to the entrance, on the left, is the venerated wooden statue of Saint

Paul, which is continually scratched by the pilgrims who want to take away splinters as relics, and, on the right, is the statue of Saint Bridget attributed to Stefano Maderno (1576-1636). Represented kneeling with her arms outstretched towards the Crucifix, where, according to tradition, Christ turned his head to her as she was deep in prayer at his feet. The Chapel also holds a venerated 13th century mosaic depicting a *Madonna and Child.*

Left: The mosaic icon of the Theotokos Hodigitria ("Mother of God, Showing the Way") in typical Byzantine style (13ᵗʰ century). In 1541, before this image, Saint Ignatius of Loyola, together with some of his followers, made their profession, thus beginning the work of the Society of Jesus. Right: The wooden crucifix (14ᵗʰ century).

19. THE SAINT LAWRENCE CHAPEL

Formerly dedicated to the Blessed Sacrament and constructed by Carlo Maderno in 1619-1620, the walls of the Saint Lawrence Chapel are decorated with eight paintings by Lanfranco, the artist of the frescoes in the lunettes and the altar pieces as well. The paintings depict scenes from the Old and New Testament; the vault bears Sibyls and Prophets by the Florentine artist, Anastasio Fontebuoni. In 1852 the restoration work following the fire was completed. Decorated by Antonio Viligiardi (1869-1936) at the beginning of the century with scenes from the life of Saint Lawrence, the vault is surrounded by angels in flight. The walls are lined with choir-stalls, designed by Calderini and executed by the Perugian engraver, A. Monteneri. Set in fanciful architectural designs are the likenesses of Saints and the two Princes of the Apostles on the back panels. Taken from the inside of the Basilica's façade the marble relief on the front of the altar can be dated between the end of the 15th century and the beginning of the 16th century. In its three shell-shaped niches appear Saint Anthony Abbot, Saint Dionysius and Saint Justine.

Right:
The altar wall with the 14th century relief, attributed to the School of Andrea Bregno.

20. THE SAINT BENEDICT CHAPEL

Built in the right transept by Luigi Poletti in 1843-1845, the Saint Benedict Chapel has a rectangular plan (17.67 metres x 8.50 metres) and a rectangular apse. Twelve ash-grey marble columns found during the excavations done in 1811-1812 in the ancient Veio district at *Isola Farnese,* .decorate its interior In 1824, the marble found was brought to Rome by Leo XII (1823-1829) and Gregory XVI (1835) donated the materials to the Basilica. Each of the 2.90 metre, 20-faceted columns has composite capitals (11 originals and 1 copy) which are decorated with stylized leaves and flowers. On a high pedestal in the niche is the statue of Saint Benedict by Pietro Tenerani (1789-1869).

Right: The statue of Saint Benedict by Pietro Tenerani (1789-1869). Opposite: The marble holy water font of Pietro Galli, sculptured for the Duchess of Beuffremount who donated it to Pius IX in 1860.

21. THE BAPTISTRY

The Baptistry, built by Arnaldo Foschini in 1930, stands in an ancient room between the Saint Julian Oratory and the Sacristy. Designed for the square in front of the Basilica, Poletti's plan replaced the small octagonal temple with a double row of columns which was never built–which. Devised in an equilateral cross plan, the centre, positioned below the level of the old Basilica, can be reached by means of steps. Supported by columns with ionic and pulvin capitals along the walls, the arches are original. Frescoes with the likenesses of Saints and the coats-of-arms of the Basilica, on the undersides of the arches, can be seen among 15th century geometric and floral motifs. The walls and floor are in polychromatic marble, while the baptismal font in the centre of the room is decorated with symbolic animals in malachite, lapis lazuli and mother-of-pearl. A frescoed frieze runs underneath the four arches. Twelve rectangular and circular compartments, among a rich leafy decoration, display busts of the Evangelists, the Doctors of the Church, God the Father, Saint Peter and Saint Paul and an unidentified Martyr-Saint. Agreed to be by the hand of Antonio da Viterbo, the frescoes can be dated from 1460 to 1465. He had previously been commissioned, in 1451-1452 by the Benedictine Order, to paint the Triptych of the Redeemer in the Church of *Santa Maria delle Grazie* in Capena, which was under the authority of the *Ostiense* monastery.

Opposite: The baptismal font.

Frescoes depicting the Apostles Peter and Paul,
attributed to Antonio da Viterbo.

22. THE SAINT JULIAN ORATORY

Known also as the Martyr Room, the Saint Julian Oratory, acts as a passageway between the transept of the Basilica and the Cloister. Despite having been repainted more than once, the frescoes along the walls, can be dated between the end of the 12th century and the beginning of the 14th century.

The Saint Julian Oratory, The Crucifixion.

The Saint Julian Oratory, The Holy Martyrs.

23. THE GREGORIAN PORTICO

The Gregorian Portico, so called because it was built by Luigi Poletti under Gregory XVI (1831-1846), is located at the northern end of the transept. Twelve columns recovered from the old Basilica were used in its construction, including the one bearing Pope Siricio's famous dedicatory inscription referring to the building of the Theodosian Basilica (19 November 390).

24. THE BELL TOWER

The Bell Tower which was erected by Luigi Poletti between 1840 and 1860 rises in the rear, in line with the axis of the Basilica. 65 metres in height, it is entirely covered with travertine marble and divided into 5 levels. On the southern and western sides of the second level – square in shape as the lower one – is the face of a clock made by Mariano Trevellini in 1863.

Progressing in clear geometric forms laid one on top of the other, square-octagon-circle,are the next three levels which follow the model of Alberti's towers, utilizing columns corresponding to the Doric-Ionic-Corinthian order. The final level takes the form of a small round monopteros temple with sixteen Corinthian columns and a high spherical vault on which is set a cross and orb. With a diameter of 6 metres the inside of the bell tower is circular in form. A spiral travertine marble staircase, with two hundred and ninety-six steps, winds its way up from the ground level to the small temple. Seven bells are suspended inside the top three levels: two of the four bells, recovered from the old Basilica, were melted down in 1863 and 1930, the remaining two, dating back to 1658, were kept until 1959, when, according to the wishes of Pope John XXIII (1958-1963), the number of bells was increased.

25. THE CLOISTER

A jewel of Cosmati art and the most significant surviving part of the ancient monastery complex, the cloister adjoins the south transept of the Basilica. Surrounded by the rectangular garden, the four ambulatories are accessible from each side. They are bound by a low podium on which rises a series of small double columns, four to each span, supporting small rounded arches which bear the splendid pediment decorated with mosaics—a unique part of the cloister— and the elaborate cornice with the heads of animals.

As a consequence of its rich and varied decoration the northern side, adjoining the Basilica, stands in contrast to the great simplicity of the other three sides. The columns possess a large variety of shapes and forms—smooth, fluted, spiral and twisted—and are very often inlaid with mosaics. The space between the small arches is attentively decorated on both the outer and inner surfaces with a succession of symbols, *flora* and *fauna* designs and monstrous, fanciful beings (leaf masks, chimeras, a face with three foreheads, "a wolf at school", etc.), which have a clear, moral intent, though lacking a general iconographical plan. Interrupted at intervals by sculptures of animals and, in some cases, human heads, the floral motif contin-

ues along the entire cornice while the coffered undersides of the arches are decorated with stylized rosettes. All these elements indicate that the author of the northern side possessed a more varied cultural background and figurative language beyond the obvious classical references from eastern and Etruscan sources, thus revealing that the cloister is the work of two different artists and two distinct periods of construction. Illustrating the beauty and the conducive nature of the place for study and prayer, the inscription on the eastern, southern and western sides of the architrave, states that the cloister was begun by the Amalfi Cardinal, Pietro di Capua, and completed by Giovanni Caetani di Ardea, the Abbot of Saint Paul's from 1212 to 1235. Dating the cloister to approximately 1208-1210 and 1230-1235 can be done by comparing the stylistic elements of the cloister to those of the cloister of Saint John Lateran from the same period. Indications lead to the belief that the northern side was built later than the other three sides and after the cloister of the Lateran (completed in 1227). It does share enough obvious similarities with that of the Lateran to identify it with the workshop of Vassalletto, in particular "Vassalletto's son", Pietro—also the author of the *Ostiense*

*Following pages:
The western side
of the cloister.*

Paschal Candlestick—who brought to completion the work on the Lateran cloister begun by his father. Many doubts still remain concerning the other sides of the cloister. However, from all indications, theories attributing the work to Pietro de Maria, author of the cloister of Sassovivo near Foligno, or more recently to the joint workmanship of Pietro Vassalletto and Nicola d'Angelo, after their completion of the Paschal Candlestick, seem totally unfounded.

*Right: Adam and
Eve tempted
by the serpent.*

*Opposite:
A chimera*

Above: Sarcophagus, 3rd century, used in the 12th century as the tomb of Pierleoni. On the front is the procession of the Muses; on the left side, Apollo playing the lyre; on the right side, the torture of Marsia.

Opposite: Statue of Pope Boniface IX, family-name Tomacelli (1389-1404), who lavished works on the Basilica; according to some, the statue was executed for the Jubilee Year 1400.

D.O   M.
BONIFA CEL-
CIVS.IX L.VS·
P.MAX   GENE
STIRPE RE
THOMA CIBO

BONIFATIO·IX·TOMACELLO
PONT·OPT·MAX
GRATI·ANIMI·MONVMENTVM
A·CASINENSI·CONGREGATIONE
OLIM·ERECTVM
MOX·TEMPORVM·INIVRIA
COLLAPSVM
LVCRETIA·TOMACELLA
COLVMNA
PALIANI·DVX
GENTILI·SVO·RESTITVIT

26. THE PICTURE GALLERY

Adjoining the sacristy and in two small rooms nearby is the Basilica Picture Gallery. It holds about forty paintings, of considerable historical-artistic value, dating from the 13th to the 19th century.

Antoniazzo Romano, Madonna with Child and Saints Benedict, Paul, Peter and Justina, tempera on wood, datable from 1480 to 1485. The presence of Saint Justina leads to the belief that the painting was commissioned to commemorate the union, in 1426, between the monastery of Saint Paul and the Congregation of Padua bearing her name.